D1596179

WOMEN WHO MARRY HOUSES

The Gothic Americans who people these vignettes command our attention — their domestic ironies constantly threaten to become cosmic absurdities. Often wry and always compassionate, McDougall skillfully blends the surreal and the homely; if Magritte had painted covers for the Saturday Evening Post, they would resemble these poems.

Carolyn Forche

I like the way Jo McDougall talks and I like the stories she tells. She sounds like no one else I know. I read her for the high fun of it.

Miller Williams

WOMEN WHO
MARRY HOUSES

Poetry by

Jo McDougall

with drawings by

Gary Buch

Coyote Love Press

The Black and Small Birds of Remorse has appeared in *The New Mexico Review*.

The Displaced and *The 875* have appeared or will appear in the *Maine Times*.

The House Facing Dahlia and *Hett Mayhew Explains* have appeared or will appear in *The Texas Review*.

The Menial appeared in the *Arkansas Times*.

Walking Down Prospect has appeared in *Intro 13*.

Distributed by the Maine Writers and Publishers Alliance, P.O. Box 7542, Portland, Maine 04112.

First Edition

Edited, Designed, and Printed by George Benington

for Charles

Walking Down Prospect

Walking down Prospect
Behind the building with the Gothic windows,
Inside me your names fly up like two quail.
When they are gone
I pull my clothes around me.
When I get home
I try to call you.
Where you are in the world now it is dark.
The phone rings into that.

Hett Mayhew Explains
Why Belton Harris Keeps his Sister Gladys Inside

Oftentimes they never know, Hett says.
It's likely Gladys never suspected
And couldn't understand what the fuss was
when the family found out
About the ears, the tail, the conversion to three toes.

Hett says when a soul's possessed
A mirror breaks.
The soul becomes the soul of a beast
And the body starts to shape itself around it.
The shattered mirror can't show
How the hair grows to cover the face.

There are, however, clues:
Trees in the yard drop their leaves out of season.
A shovel moves.
All the doors in the house slam shut at noon.

Hett says you may notice that,
And the cats with no tails
That come to your house on Tuesdays.
Or you may not.

Hett believes
Gladys Harris never noticed
And doesn't understand why she can't go out
Why somebody burned her shoes
How it is the woman in Pine Bluff
Makes all her clothes

Women Who Marry Houses

Have lost husbands
To time or to other women.
They look for smaller houses
With hipped roofs.
They move into neighborhoods with large trees.
Women who marry houses
Are fond of the dark
When the house cracks its knuckles.

A Lady Charged with Involuntary Manslaughter Says

It will go bad
But you won't know when.
Say some night,
Driving fast along the flats of Kansas,
Not too fast,
Thinking back,
    Brushing your hair at a summer dock,
    Taking off your clothes
    Pouring a scotch

The car takes a hill, reaches the top.
Something there, maybe not,
The shadow of a cloud, cast by the moonlight,
Or something in your headlights, kneeling.

The 875

In Gillett, a town in Arkansas
On January twelfth of every year
Eight hundred and seventy-five citizens
Buy tickets for platters of raccoon and rice.

Trappers bring the coons in, skinned,
Three legs gone,
One ending in the little hand
To make certain that no dog or cat
Has been run in.

Becoming Invisible
(a found poem from The Archive of Arkansas Folklore)

It is possible to become invisible.
Follow a few simple steps.
First, you catch a toad.
Put it in a clay planter,
The type with a hole in the bottom.
The first full moon
Take it out to the grave yard.
Find a grave with an ant hill on it.
Put the toad on the ant hill;
Cover it with the pot.
The next full moon
Go back and get the toad's bones.
Take them home and stand in front of a mirror.
Place the bones
One at a time in your mouth
Until you find the one
That makes you invisible.

There are 2,000 bones in a frog.

The Professor of Chinese Dialects
in a Small University Town in Ohio

Hears the 5:15 from Akron
Slide toward the single strip
Of the tiny airport.
Standing at the kitchen table
He makes himself one drink,
Unfolds and folds his paper.
After supper his wife goes into the bedroom
Goes naked to bed
Goes slowly to sleep.

The man sits in the next room, translating Li Po.
He does not see the moon that Li Po speaks of
Or the woman.
Under the eaves the night birds
Rustle like taffeta.

She Confesses Her Love

For a man with a bald spot.
The bald spot maddens, aggressive
As the stump that hangs out of a sleeve.
In summer the sun plays a one-note fortissimo upon it
In winter it ices over
She scatters suet on it
Grackles sweep down
She puts up a scarecrow for it
And a little canopy against the sleet

    Then we strut down the sidewalk together
    Sleek oiled crows
    What panoply! What noise!
    The grackles clattering, clicking on the bald spot
    The magpies circling for the glint
    We put up a red umbrella
    A toucan rides on it
    Bumping kisses and directions to everyone we meet

But this is absurd.
Isn't this absurd?
Tomorrow I step out of this scene.
October now. First signs of sleet.
I will tell you what I want
I want to become a grackle
Beak and foot

13

Night Flight, Delta # 481

We are rising up from Boston
Heading for Bangor, Maine.
The flight attendant's smile
Hangs before us.
A tube and a mask make circles in the air.

Once, in New Orleans, on Decatur Street
You drew yourself into a ring of chalk.
You danced to the skittering music from Mollie's Bar,
Clicking the change in your pockets like castanets.
You stepped over the circle and disappeared
Into the crowd.
I have looked for you —
By rivers,
In depots, on loading docks.
A man on skates,
A man bending to pet his cat,
A man running across a darkening street
Is finally you.
He is not.

I turn out my reading light.
Pretending to touch your arm
I touch the window beside me,
Cold as it passes through the stars.

14

Admission

On the outskirts of a carnival near Pueblo
A fox and a shrike amble by.
In a quarter-turn the fox becomes a man,
The shrike a woman.
He smiles through his rusty mustache
He takes her elbow
Her polished nails curl inward.
She rests her arm in the crook of his. They enter
The yellow and mad lights.

Dropping a Line

Six months have passed
And no word.
I am playing hopscotch on the page.
I skip everything I need to tell you.
If I cross a line or step on a stone
I am lost. I will not get into Heaven.
Therefore, I do not say Come back
It is dark

I send you this letter
Without a line you can use.

Silly Women

When death sees a silly woman
He ambles over
And asks her to dance
If she says Thank you no
He puts his hand on her shoulder
Turns her around
Teaches her an old step
Or two

Death likes silly women
Who believe the names he gives them
Who will be ready when he wants to go
Who dance a little closer than they should

Reporting Back

There has been an accident.
A bridge has broken. The water under it
Has taken a bus, a car, a truck.
For days we watch a picture
Of the one survivor
Who fell with his truck tucked around him, two hundred feet,
Bounced off a passing freighter,
Was pulled back.
The man will not talk with reporters
Or answer his phone

Some who see what they see will never tell
Say they don't remember
Say what somebody said they said.
Buy this man a drink.
Ask him
What did you think of going down?
Hydrangeas? Your mother? A fox?
"A fox," he says.

To Her

I get up
From the cold bed,
Open the door.
Someone with his hand at my back
Pushes me into a room with a bed
Where I am sleeping.
The woman in the bed will not wake up
Although I beat on her chest
A long time.

For Stephen, Who Owns a Bag of My Cut Fingernails, Carried in the Mouth of an Eel Who Swam the Caddo

On out fifteen miles past Wabbaseka,
Past Seaton, Gethsemane, and Plain,
He and I grew up neighbors in houses
Facing Danner's Bayou. White plantation houses,
Splendid except for needing paint.

Except for occasional killings,
Times were quiet.
One night the police broke into Mama Laura's place—
The Dew-Drop-Inn on 3rd, where the black people went.
They found where a fire had been, and bones.
She got the bones, they said, out of graves.
Then my grandfather told me about Vera,
Used to work for my mother. He said that's where
They all learn, from Vera.

We went to her place and hollered til she came out,
Scraping the wash house door.
We begged her to tell us. She told us no;
She said my mama would run her off,
And we were babies only.
We were ten, and twelve; we loved the way she smelled;
We wanted to know all about the bones.
She said we were evil children.
She said to come back in an hour.

What she did then was strange.

22

All through high school we met at the bayou,
Early, before flies.
We tried to do what she'd taught us. We got scared.
One morning in your senior year,
In April, the moon in its last quarter,
We got it. Except we neither one of us knew the woman
We made appear.
We scraped the twigs together
And watched them burn.

I knew we had the power.
I said we ought to tell Vera
Who'd quit us and gone home.
She died in middle August, during drouth.
Neighbors who went in for the body
Found in the top of her closet
A little coffin
Not much bigger than a shoe box
With owls' feet and a few thin sticks.

He went to college in Missouri.
I buried Mama; went to work for the bank. I wrote him
Drouth was ruining Danner's Bayou.

We never got married. It seemed as though we would.
One day I came to be in St. Louis.
Gazing in a store front, I saw his reflection
In back of mine.
No accident, he said. He caused it.

We often used the power after that.
That time we met in Bonn, that was my doing;
That time in Platte, as the traffic light changed.

It's two years since I saw him last.
Crossing a street in Memphis,
I enter a bar in Portland, Maine.
He is nowhere around.
I freeze to think what's happening in that bayou,
The three sticks crossing,
The owl dropping a stone where the sticks cross.
The awful joy of it. The tooth, the nail. The blazing.
Looking for him, I circle through the bar.
I look in a mirror.
The person I see does not have my face,
And backs away.

Dancing Man

The music in Mick's Bar
Is three parts smoke and one part hard down blues.
The man who brought me drinks bourbon shots and beer.
A woman shouts in the next booth
Play something for me Play something slow for me.

One of the men on the dance floor
Has on your brown hat,
Three guinea feathers in the hat band.
You are in Mexico, or Greece.

I would leave with him,
Let him do whatever he wanted to do
If he would keep the hat on.

On a Sunday Night in Hattiesburg

A man clicks an index open
To a certain address in Baltimore.
A woman half as tall as a thumbnail
Hops out.
Mistaking her for a silverfish,
He scoots her off the desk.
He learns the next day
His friend has died in Baltimore,
A woman whose husband is charged
With killing his wife.
The husband swears that she died in her sleep
That she cried out once
That bruises on her body
Came from inside
Came from the broken bones.

The House Facing Dahlia

In the house next door facing Dahlia, Ardeliah Soames—
Whose front yard flourished with sunflower whirligigs,
Cement flamingoes, and a cat she called Malone—
died today.

Saturdays there had come a black boy mowing the lawn,
Each Saturday for three years or so.
She called the boy Floyd. His name was Foster.

Today, in a tie and suit
Foster came after they took Mrs. Soames away.
He stood on the step and watched the whirligigs turn.
He reached for some weeds and bunched them.
Then walking squatted not to soil his suit,
He weeded both sides of the walk.
Malone lifted his head and watched,
Said nothing to him and went back to sleep.

Foster took a sunflower as he left
And one of the pink flamingoes,
Still inclined and delicate
Under his arm.

The Black and Small Birds of Remorse

Come in the cool hours
One by one
To perch on the backs of chairs.
Anywhere you are trying to start over —
Tossing green salad, changing white sheets —
They glide in of a sudden,
Shift from foot to foot.

Harlot Hag Dry Harpie

A woman from Opelousas
Went to live
With a barker from Royal American Shows
Who had lived with an alligator lady, and Siamese twins.
So the woman from Opelousas
Would sometimes paint a harelip on herself,
Tape down an eyelid, paint her nose black, sleep on all fours.
Once she tied her ankle to her thigh
And hopped over to him and did his will.

On those nights he could go on forever
On those nights he'd chant a crawling song:
Pomegranate sequin dove my harlot hag dry harpie
As he would cradle her head against his face
He'd painted purple for her
And he would cry.
She'd lick his tears he'd rock her
Jesus Mother Mary Martha Tessie Christ Lord Love

Emerson County Shaping Dream

Any girl in Emerson County
Knows what dreams are for:
Daddy in the shape of a rich boy.
She chooses him who chooses her,
Dreamed in the shape of his mama.
Both houses are happy
If the girl is pretty,
If the boy's daddy owns some land: flat, not rolling land;
A hillside farm won't get you anywhere.
If there's money enough, no one will say
How the boy goes after his mama with a knife,
How the girl sleeps with her daddy.
After the wedding
There will be parties on wide porches.
One night a man from a neighboring county
May get a little drunk.
They will begin to meet
At the Albert Pick, or the Claridge.
Nobody will mention this, either.

Alice B. Toklas and Moon
(from a letter to Gertrude)

It was anger with you at some slight
Made me stomp out to the garden
To look at the moon half-sitting on our house.
The night felt like fine porcelain
Left standing in cool windows.
I examined the moon from behind.
I got round the other side.
I got on the moon and rode.

I could hear you calling Alice Alice
As the moon rose.
Don't worry; I'm fine. I'm waited on
By long, soft girls.
I have a garden of my own.
I've worked out the colors as you do words:
Green upon green
And the shock of one red canna.

My astors bloom large as plates.
(Don't forget you've invited twelve for Sunday next.)
This week I'll send you astors
Just the color for the hall,
And in the fall I'll send you the seed of the canna,
Microscopic, prolific,
Black as Sunday shoes.

The Displaced

He sat on my bed.
He lit a cigarette.
I said Excuse me but how did you get in?
He said through the mail slot
And where did I keep the Scotch?

The next morning
He came back with a china suitcase—white,
The state of Maine emblazoned with roses.
That was all in 1965.
Today I promised
I would call him Al.

The Menial

Each woman keeps another woman—
Old, painted, with spittle on her chin
Who comes through a small gate when we call her
To cook, to clean our teeth
To suckle our young
Even to bed down in our names
To make love in our names
To have our children
She will do almost anything except
Dig in the ground a rectangle
Sink into that a box with a lid
Climb into that naked

Something, Anything

The way Mrs. Jensen slams the window shut
In the apartment above says
I'm here.
Also
Krebbs at the bench on Maple and 3rd
Showing off his new teeth,
Irma Bagley swiping a dirty menu
From the Cafe Royale
To show Mrs. Payton who's never been
Anywhere.

Pilgrims, we may not make it.

36

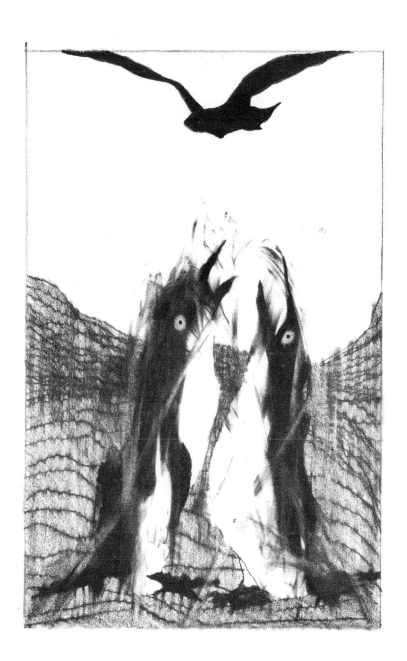

photo by John Peel

Jo McDougall, a native of the Arkansas Delta, now lives in the Ozark Mountains at Fayetteville, as well as Rodgers, where she has worked in the writer's workshops at the University of Arkansas. She has been awarded a fellowship in poetry at the Stonecoast Writers' Conference, University of Southern Maine.